Echoes *Out of My* Heart

MARGARET V. BUCKMIRE

CrossBooks™
A Division of LifeWay
1663 Liberty Drive
Bloomington, IN 47403
www.crossbooks.com
Phone: 1-866-879-0502

© 2012 Margaret V. Buckmire. All rights reserved.

No part of this book may be reproduced, stored in a retrieval system, or transmitted by any means without the written permission of the author.

Scripture taken from the New King James Version. Copyright 1979, 1980, 1982 by Thomas Nelson, inc. Used by permission. All rights reserved.

First published by CrossBooks 02/10/2012

ISBN: 978-1-4627-1337-0 (sc)
ISBN: 978-1-4627-1338-7 (e)

Printed in the United States of America

This book is printed on acid-free paper.

Any people depicted in stock imagery provided by Thinkstock are models, and such images are being used for illustrative purposes only.

Certain stock imagery © Thinkstock.

Because of the dynamic nature of the Internet, any web addresses or links contained in this book may have changed since publication and may no longer be valid. The views expressed in this work are solely those of the author and do not necessarily reflect the views of the publisher, and the publisher hereby disclaims any responsibility for them.

ACKNOWLEDGEMENT

I thank all those who encouraged me in expository and creative writing, and gave me inspiration. Thanks also to Dr. Lizette I. Westney who assisted in the review of the manuscript. This book is posthumously dedicated to Graham A. Stroude who first motivated me to write short stories during my teenage years. I would also like to dedicate this book to my daughter Michelle and grand daughter Micha Maria Keens-Douglas. But above all I thank God for conviction and inspiration to write.

...For out of the abundance of the heart
the mouth speaks (Matthew 12:34 NKJV).

Contents

A GARDEN OF CLOUDS

I looked out the window of Pan Am Flight 219,
And saw the wonder of a magnificent scene
Of a beautiful garden of tranquil clouds,
And I remembered God created this wonderful world.

Above and below the sky and water look blue,
Clouds in the middle are many shapes and hues,
Some so thick, one can't see through;
The wonder of this tells me God's Word is true.

The sun shines in all its radiance,
And illuminates the clouds in the distance
As they stand still and out of reach.
Oh! What a lesson they teach.

In flight to the Caribbean
I marveled at God's majestic creation
For no matter where I stand,
I see tapestry of His hand.

I see the land, the sand, and the ocean,
Which blend with the sky and the clouds,
And God's creation speaks very loud,
As Flight 219 prepares to touch the ground.

A RARE ROSE
First Elder, MSDA Church

Pamela Palmer—a flower in my life.
As a flower in the garden of life,
You are a rare rose.
Beautiful and strong,
Kind and gracious.
Your joy within is spontaneous,
And quickly flows out
To others who may be in doubt.
You leave a fragrance behind
That will last a lifetime.
Thank you for your loving, caring ways.

A MOTHER'S LOVE

A mother's love is so hard to explain.
'Tis deep emotion, passion and pain.
'Tis filled with joy and abiding love,
Which only comes from God above.

'Tis a guiding hand and a shining light
That gives direction in every phase,
From birth throughout the years,
That's often filled with many tears.

And when life's trials assail,
It will calm her children's fears,
And will bring comfort in weakness,
Until God manifests His goodness.

A mother's love has no boundary
For it ascends the highest height,
And descends the lowest valley,
And extends throughout eternity.

Oh! How sweet the joys
Of a mother's love.
Children don't understand
The guiding of a mother's hand
That's filled with knowledge and wisdom,
Yet a mother's love will endure
'Till time is no more.

AN OLD CLAY HOUSE

I live in an old house of clay,
'Cause I'm not here to stay.
I don't need a mansion fair,
'Cause one day I'll fly away.

The hinges, bolts and screws,
Oh! How they get so loose
From wear and tear by wind and rain,
So I must keep it maintained.

In this old house of clay,
The paint just peels away,
And it always needs repair,
For the house shows much decay.

This old house is not my final home,
You see, Jesus is building my mansion,
And one day I'll fly beyond the beyond,
To that house not made by hands.

My spirit, the breath in my nostril,
Speaks from this earthen vessel,
That longs to be free from pain
To be where it'll forever reign.

Jesus said, "I will come again."
Lord, help me board that glory train,
So I can reach my final home,
And hear the sweet sound, "Welcome!"

ASPIRATIONS TO FLY

I admire all creatures that fly,
Even a beetle or a busy bee
That goes about its journey
Working to make honey.

I admire all creatures that soar as they fly.
I stop and watch them rise and rise,
As if reaching for the sky!
They help me hold my head up high,
And think of One afar, but yet so nigh.

I admire all creatures that fly,
Sometimes I pause and wonder why,
For each one tells a wondrous story
Of purpose and harmony.

As human beings we too must fly,
And quest for knowledge beyond the sky,
For we have the greatest story to tell,
That will save others from a fiery hell.

As human beings we too must fly,
And let the Master lead as we try
To aspire to make heaven our goal,
As we see Bible Prophecies unfold.

AWAKE! TELL THE STORY

Awake! I'll awake and tell the story,
That Jesus left his home in glory,
And was born in a lowly stable,
For there was no room with the noble.

Awake! I'll awake and tell the story,
How Jesus healed the sick
And the blind He made to see,
And how He fed the hungry,
And calmed the angry sea.

Awake! I'll awake and tell the world,
That Jesus gives peace to one's soul.
He is a shelter from life's storms,
And water to the thirsty and worn.

Awake! I'll awake and tell the story,
Of His pain and agony,
When He walked the streets of Galilee,
And died on a cross at Calvary.

Awake! I'll awake and tell the story,
Of Jesus' love and mercy
That removed the curse of sin
So you and I can live with Him.

Oh yes! I'll arise and join the Gospel Band,
And tell of His incarnation and crucifixion,
His resurrection and glorification,
And His ascension to make intercession,
To secure my redemption and salvation.

Oh yes! I'll arise. I'll arise and sing,
Sing praises to the Heavenly King.
I'll sing about justice and mercy,
While telling this "old, old story",
That Jesus died to save you and me.

ARE YOU TELLING THE STORY?

ADRIAN T. WESTNEY — A TRIBUTE

The life of Adrian T. Westney
Had a purpose and a destiny
In service to God and humanity
As he traveled this pilgrim journey.

In pursuit of learning at all levels,
He reached for excellence in the highest degree,
Which he imparted to others as he labored
As Pastor, Teacher, Administrator and Counselor.

He worked with diligence and dignity,
Physically, spirituality and with family.
He sprinkled everything with love and humility
That showed depth in his spirituality.

He "set his face like a flint,"
Therefore, God gave him wisdom to think
How to bring peace and reconciliation
In many difficult situations.

He "stood like a (mighty) brave",
Thoughtful, and caring in many ways
To help nurture others to learn
Lessons to reach God's Kingdom.

He labored in mission here
Which touched lives everywhere,
But focused on a home Over There
That one day they might share.

He saw time rapidly marching on,
And soon we'll hear the loud trumpet sound,
When Jesus shall burst through the clouds.
Again we'll meet Adrian T. Westney,
And forever enjoy ceaseless ages of eternity.

J. GLEN ROBERTS - A TRIBUTE
Pastor, Metropolitan SDA Church

Pastor J. Glen Roberts,
I miss your inspirational sermons;
And "Call to Worship" t'was second to none
Which gave me glimpses of heaven!

Memories of you will live on,
How you preached with conviction,
And moved souls to compassion,
To seek their own salvation.

In reflecting on your mission
How you gave guidance and direction,
I always envision a celebration
Of a joyous congregation.

In my mind's eyes,
I still see your lovely smile
That twinkles in your eyes,
As you "zip" across the aisles.

I thank God for you,
And the many years you shepherded
This great congregation at Metropolitan,
As you complete your earthly mission.

I'll remember you always.
So enjoy your retirement years,
And I'll see you on the Other Side,
Where I'll forever abide. Praise God!

MARTIN LUTHER KING, JR.
(A Man on a Mission)

Who was Martin Luther King, Jr.?
He was a preacher and a great orator,
So in speech and eloquence he did not falter,
When he spoke with persuasion and flair.

Martin Luther King had many goals
One of which was to win souls.
He gave people vision so they might see
God's amazing grace and glory.

Martin Luther King had dignity,
And so he wanted all to have equality.
He gave us faith and courage to endure
Life's obstacles so we can soar.

In quest for freedom, he did advocate,
Peace and non-violence in every state.
Martin, a man of great principles,
Was truly one of God's disciples.

On many issues Martin spoke,
And faithfully he bore a heavy yoke,
As he lived by faith each day,
And never ceased to pray.

In battles Martin did not yield
To the pain and sorrows he did feel
In life's trials of ups and downs
For God was his solid ground.

Martin Luther King was Black,
So pride for his people he did not lack.
For Black and White he had a dream ...
But, his untimely death, he had not seen.

Martin Luther King was our friend,
Who fought for freedom to the end,
And gave this nation inspiration,
As he stood up for truth and freedom.

Who was Martin Luther King, Jr.?
He was a drum major for peace.
He was a drum major for freedom.
He was a drum major for justice,
He was a drum major for Jesus!

ROBERT EDWARDS,

Executive Pastor
Metropolitan SDA Church

Well, Pastor Edwards,
You must go forward.
You made the plans
And God carries out the action.
And though you may not understand,
You must trust His guiding hand
For He sees the grand design
And has a better plan.

Your short tenure with us
Has been so infectious.
The fragrance you left behind
Will surely last a lifetime.

We will miss:
Your vivacious, high-spirited personality
That shows depth in your spirituality.
Your words of inspiration and admonition
To parents at baby dedication
To help in childrearing direction,
And interpersonal relations.

We will miss:
Your words of encouragement,
Administration and management,
Your enthusiastic, energetic, effervescent,
Invincible, vibrant, personality
That is so refreshing like cool sparkling water
In summer humidity.

We, the members of the Fifty Plus Association,
Will remember you in prayer
As you labor for the Master over there,
Knowing well that God sees the big picture
And therefore, outlines the future.

So today, we give you words like petals of roses
While you can still smell fragrance.
We wish you success and continued endurance
And may God's countenance
Always shine upon you and your family.
Thank you and God's rich blessings.

Margaret V. Buckmire on behalf of Members of the Fifty Plus Association
Metropolitan SDA Church
February 19, 2011

THE DINOSAUR

Out of the depths of the clear blue sea,
A big, ugly creature appeared to me.
It began to roar as it rushed ashore,
And the children shouted, "It's a dinosaur!"

In the surging tide it moved up and down.
Where in the world has this creature grown?
I looked in wonder with an awesome frown,
But the children were spellbound!

On the horizon a ship came in sight.
It moved swiftly to assist in our plight,
But the voices of the children made uproar!
Awe! And the dinosaur quickly went below.

The ship turned its bow towards the horizon,
Against the beautiful sun that was setting,
And we looked at the stern of that majestic ship,
While our thoughts were on the dinosaur's trip.

The ship slowly went out of view,
And the children dispersed to only a few,
But, we will always remember what we saw,
Oh! What a big, ugly dinosaur!

Well, all creatures big and small,
God, the Creator, made them all,
But today, we can't find the dinosaurs,
Yet they are part of the fossil record,
That shows the wonder of nature.

(1986. This scene was so vivid in my mind's eye as if standing on Grand Anse Beach witnessing this drama)

THE EAGLE

Up high in the clear blue sky
I see an eagle fly;
As its wings gracefully glide,
I begin to wonder why.

The eagle soars high
Above the stormy clouds
And views the motion of a storm's eye
And then makes a decision to hide.

It then finds a hollow cleft
In a mighty rock,
And with its feet it clings,
And covers its head with its wings.

While the storm is raging,
It holds steadfast, waiting —
Knowing this tempest will pass,
For no storm can forever last.

Then eagle continues to fly
Against the beauty of the sky,
And travels for many miles,
Then rests 'till another sunrise.

Its vision is stronger than human eye,
So it views its prey up high from the sky
And swiftly plunges many miles
And seizes its prey by surprise.

Have you ever heard ...?
The eagle is King of the Birds,
Who builds a mighty fortress
To withstand life's greatest tempests.

The eagle is majestic and strong,
And has power, grace and charm,
So it makes a lovely Coat of Arms
For many nations large and small.

The eagle is one of God's creations,
That possesses lots of wisdom,
That shows God's majestic and creative power,
In the wonderful world of nature.

ETERNITY IS HEAVEN

I'm counting down to eternity,
As I listen to the drum beat of history,
And see the signs unfold,
As told by the prophets of old.

The nations of the earth are perplexed,
And men everywhere are wond'ring,
What will be next
As the hourglass keeps filling?

Jesus said, "Behold, I come quickly."
Yet, many are not ready
To meet their eternal destiny,
Where they'll spend eternity.

I must be ready for earth's closing battle,
When Jesus will change earth's title,
And build the New Jerusalem,
After the war of Armageddon.

Oh yes! I am counting,
And I'm busy preparing,
Can't wait for the trumpet sound,
When Jesus comes in the clouds,
With angels singing "Glory,
Glory to God Almighty."

Oh! I don't want to miss heaven,
I heard it's a land far, far beyond,
With many, many mansions
That are not made by hand.

In that glorious homeland,
I'll see Jasper and Topaz,
While walking on the Sea of Glass,
And behold streets paved in pure gold,
Just as the Bible has told.

I'll see Sapphire and Emeralds,
Pearls and Beryl,
Amethyst and Sardius,
And they're all made by Jesus!

So I must be ready to meet my Creator,
To live in a land without fear and war,
There I'll sing "Glory, Halleluiah,"
Just praising my God forever.

FLOWERS IN THE GARDEN OF LIFE

We are flowers in the garden of life,
All planted to blossom in Christ,
We need God's tender care
Every day along life's way.

We're His handiwork of art,
Carefully designed to play a part
In the garden made for man
To complete God's Master Plan.

Each one's uniquely structured,
And "wonderfully made" by the Creator,
To add beauty in life's garden
Until transplanted to Eden.

In the morning we bloom so bright,
In the evening we wither into the night
And there we lie dormant
To be awakened by that Bright Light.

FORCES OF NATURE

The wonder of it –
See the awesome power of nature,
It captures our imagination,
And in amazement we gaze
At its mysterious force and power.

The wonder of it –
Who understands how the wind billows?
As it swirls round-and-round and continues to roar.
Only God, the Omnipotent, for He is in control,
And can say, "Peace, be still!"
And the wind quickly obeys His will.

The wonder of it –
See the boiling volcanic lava,
What can cool such thick, hot fire?
Not even the depth of ocean water,
But God in His awesome power,
Can put out any raging fire.

The wonder of it –
Look at the mighty ocean,
Such expanse of water can cover every land,
But its command is to stand behind small grains of sand,
While the sea creatures capture our imagination,
And they're all controlled by that Mighty Hand.

The sea roars with might and fury,
From wind and current we don't understand,
Its waves caress small grains of sand,
Yet, never overtakes the land,
And the wonder of it all,
It's controlled by God's Almighty Hand.

GOD ANSWERS PRAYER (GAP)

"I know not by what means, though rare",
But I truly know God answers prayer.
Day-by-day I tell Him how I feel,
And to His will I simply yield.

Sometimes I feel too weak to toil,
But on God I'll always call,
I lean on His "Everlasting Arms"
And my fears He always calms.

Often when I'm unable to fend,
On God I always can depend.
I whisper a few words in prayer,
And He quickly lights the way.

God is always standing by,
Just waiting to hear my cry,
And He always comforts and cheers
With a song to smooth the way.

GOD CARES

Deep in the forest I venture,
Into that open Book of Nature
That reveals God's creative power
In every crevice and corner.

The sprawling sycamore tree,
Tells a beautiful Bible story,
Of a little man's determination
To climb it and gain salvation.

Running vines are everywhere,
Inter-twining in strong embrace,
That tells of God's love and care
For His creation so fair.

Birds play in the trees,
And sing among the leaves.
They bask in a lovely world
Created for them with love.

This vast Book of Nature,
Tells much about our Heavenly Father
Who provides for all His creatures
And sustains them by his power.

Here I see God's amazing love
Even though I'm so alone;
In this wild and vast wilderness,
There's God's love and tenderness,
For God cares!

THE GREAT I AM

When I'm weary, I go to the Rock,
When I'm weak, I cling to the Vine,
When I'm thirsty, I go to the Living Water,
When I'm hungry, I go to the Bread of Life,
When I'm lost, I go to the Good Shepherd,
When I'm in darkness, I go to the Light,
When I'm perplexed, I go back to the Beginning
    and the End –
The Alpha and the Omega –
    The Great I Am!

GRENADA — THE ISLE OF SPICE

When God created Grenada,
He placed in that part of nature,
Some special spices of sweet fragrance,
So we can have the "Isle of Spice",
And that's Grenada. Oh! It's a paradise!

I remember lofty mountains, rolling plains,
Dense rain forests, and sugar cane,
And the smell of fragrant spices: Cinnamon, ginger, clove,
Bay leaf, tanker bean, cocoa bean, turmeric, nutmeg, pimento,
And the taste of flavorful mangoes!

Oh! How I remember
Our picturesque and exotic Grenada,
As I live in beautiful America.
Oft times my mind embraces,
The constellation of a starry night,
And the magnificence of a tropical moon,
Shining down on the sleepy lagoon,
As I eat at Nutmeg Restaurant,
Or while swimming in the ocean at night.

I remember crystal-clear seawater,
And white, shining sand of Grand Anse Beach,
As I stroll in the cool sea breeze,
And see the mystical wonder of a tropical sunset,
Before the night bids me come to rest.

But then I hear the wind whisper,
"Oh Grenada! Where are my sons and daughters
Who have traveled to cold, distant lands
In search of adventure and higher education?
Oh! My children return! Let's hold hands,
For I'm still lovely and full of charm."

(I would like to thank Gloria Charles for her encouragement and persuasion to have me write this poem.)

IN TIMES LIKE THESE

In times like these, I need a Pilot,
Who rides the wind like a chariot,
Who walks on the clouds,
Who lights the moon, the sun, and the stars,
Who says to the ocean –
"You've come thus far!"

So when life's storms begin to blow,
I have a hiding place to go
Where I feel safe and secure
'Til those billows cease to roar.

As the battles of life rage on,
And the enemy seems so strong,
I'll remember, God sits on His Throne,
And has everything in control!

God is my anchor, my fortress
In life's raging tempests;
In Him I find peace and rest,
Waiting for His mighty conquest.

In times like these, I'll remember,
God is my shelter and strong tower,
God is my shield and protector,
God is my Judge and Defender,
And in Him I'm safe forever.

JESUS IS JOY
PART I

In the midst of life's trials,
When I'm deep in the valley,
Or high on the mountaintop,
Or when there seems to be no hope,
Though the night is spent,
And sleep does not come,
I'll still continue to pray, and
And remember Jesus is my joy!

In the midst of life's trials,
When barely hanging on,
I'll still sing a great song
That will cheer me along,
And will remind me I'm not alone,
And I feel well at home
Knowing Jesus is still my Joy!

JESUS IS JOY
PART II

J. J is for Jesus!
The "Rose of Sharon,"
The "Prince of Peace,"
The "Lilly of the Valley,"
The "Morning Star."
He could not stay in a tomb.

O. O is for over!
'Cause at Calvary
All his suffering ends,
Where He died to save me.

Y. Y is for yes!
Say yes to Jesus,
For He is love, joy, peace, hope,
And so much more.
He's everything!

ASK, SEEK, KNOCK

Cast: Three children
Large letters – **A S K**

A. **A** is for ask. One day I asked Jesus, "Who am I?" He replied, "You are a child of God." In Him you have eternal life.

S. **S** is for seek. One day I sought and obeyed the Lord, and He said all the things I need will be given unto me.

K. **K** is for knock. One day Jesus knocked and I opened the door. He said, "I Am the Door." Enter in and be saved from sin.

"Ask and it shall be given you, seek and you shall find, knock and it shall be opened unto you." Matthew 7:7 (NKJV).

LOVE IN MOTION

Oh! I love thee in so many ways -
A warm smile,
A gentle kiss,
A strong hug,
A thoughtful gift,
A tender touch,
A loving look,
Or, I may just hush!

Oh! I love thee in so many ways.
Each morning I open my eyes; that's love,
I kneel and pray to begin the day; that's love.

Love's principles are always in motion,
That's why God had a plan,
And He put love in action
In the form of a man - His Son.
So how do I love thee?
It's always in motion.

LOVE HAS AN END

I reach out continuously,
To hold you in empty dreams,
To touch your face,
And feel your warm embrace.

I listen and shed tears,
Over a sentimental song,
And have a million celebrations,
Of love I cherished for so long,
And recurring dreams that are gone.

Loving you was not by chance,
For God always has a mission
To complete His Master Plan,
For He sets the race in advance,
And knows each foolish decision.

In the deep recesses of your heart,
You knew you could not impart,
True love to me from the start,
And now there is an emptiness
Our hearts cannot dismiss.

My spirit, my heart, my soul,
Still cry out to hold you some more,
But, I must let you go,
For time, O time, is no more.

And now I say good-bye to youthful love,
And hope you discern God's purpose;
For though we took a different course,
With humility, repentance and love,
We can both make it to Heaven above.

LOVING THE WIND -RAIN IN SPRING

You bring me joy
When it seems I had lost it all;
You cause my heart to sing
A love melody deep within.

My love is endless,
And it will not die;
'Tis renewed each time I try
To sing love's soft refrains;
It blossoms all over again.

I see the flowers bloom
Out of winter's sleepy gloom,
When I taste the wind's gentle kiss
And wait for a moment of bliss.

I kiss the wind's fingertips,
And hold my breath to kiss its lips;
Then, in its arms it holds me so
Lovingly and won't let me go.

The wind's arms enfold me so strong,
And allow my feelings to carry on,
For only my heart can attest,
To the joy the wind makes me express.

I love to feel the wind's body sway,
For there I'll always stay,
Knowing it's spring time again,
I'll sing love's sweet refrain,
And hope it'll never rain.

MY LOVE

Oh! My love,
I love you so much;
Let me hold you in my arms,
For they are long and strong.

I want you to take my love,
For it has no end,
I'll guide you along life's journey,
And I'll feed you when hungry.

I'll give you crystal clear water,
That will never, never run dry,
That spouts high from a fountain,
To help you climb life's mountains,

Look deep into my eyes,
And you'll see beyond the sky.
Gaze straight into my face,
There you'll see amazing grace,
And I'll hold you in my embrace.

Oh! How I want your heart,
You were mine from the start,
I know every part of your body,
Externally and internally.

I know the way you walk,
And even the way you talk,
I know when you're hungry,
And even when you're thirsty.

Please, let me hold your hand,
I'll walk you through this vast land,
I'll stay close to you when no one is around,
And I won't ever let you down,
I'll always keep you in my sight,
And I'll be in every battle you fight.

I'll be there for you to lean on my breast,
When you're tired and need to rest,
I'll be with you in the morning,
Evening and mid-night,
I'll always hold you so tight.

I'll be watching you,
When sleeping and waking,
Oh girl! You are the "apple of my eye"
And you are always on my mind.

Please don't ever go away,
Or let your thoughts even stray,
For I'm in your life to stay,
Oh! My love,
My love is endless,
It will never die.

And when this life on earth is o'er,
I'll renew your life to last forever,
For I'm taking it and you with me,
To spend eternity beyond the sky,
For I'm Eternal.

Oh Yes! I'm your Father, your mother,
Your husband, your lover,
Your brother, your sister.
Oh yes! I'm your Maker!

MERCY, COMPASSION AND FAITHFULNESS

Lord, I come to you for grace,
Since it's abundantly free,
And each day new **mercies** I see,
To help me run this set journey.

Lord, I come to you for **compassion,**
It's to be my close companion,
And because it's new each morning,
Your praises this day I will sing.

Lord, help me to be always thankful,
Because of your **great faithfulness**,
For each day your promises are renewed,
Lord, help me always to stay close to you.

ONCE ON AN ISLAND

Once on an island I walked unpaved streets,
And spoke to everyone I would meet,
But some people refused to speak,
Although they walked the same streets.

Once on an island I remember,
One thing that caused such behavior,
To share the precious gift of words,
'Twas because of pride; some felt too proud.

God's Word is immortal and never fails,
And God hates pride, no matter how small,
For pride precedes a fall that takes one down,
Due to a lack of knowledge and wisdom.

We must teach our children well,
So they can have a good story to tell,
For we're made by One Heavenly Father,
Who loves us and tells us to love one another.

Throughout history God's Word prevails;
Our journey here is just a tale,
And we must stand before God's judgment,
To give an account of our earthly deportment.

ON THE WINGS OF PRAYER

On the wings of prayer,
I take my flight each day
To meet my Savior anywhere,
For my Lord is always there.

On the wings of prayer,
My soul rises above life's cares,
Whether it's morning or at noonday,
For God always has an open ear.

On the wings of prayer,
I ease my soul from despair,
And picture scenes beyond the "Milky Way"
And then I remember there's a God who cares.

On the wings of prayer,
My heart soars above sorrows and tears,
So I see beyond this present sphere,
When I remember my Savior is near.

On the wings of prayer,
I listen for a song of cheer,
And then I hear my Savior say,
"Be still, my child, I'm here."

So on the wings of prayer,
I'll soar high in the air,
Knowing my battles God will fight
As I continue to take my flight.

ONE PEOPLE, DESTINED FOR ETERNITY

In Christ we are one people,
Striving to reach one destiny,
In that celestial city of beauty,
Where we will spend eternity.

We must tell the Good News,
So lost souls may also choose
Salvation that's rich and free to all,
If they would heed the Savior's call.

On Christ we fix our hearts each day,
Seeking guidance from Him in prayer,
And await the Spirit's command,
To lead someone to salvation.

Since we are in Christ,
And we are one people, with one destiny,
Love and unity we display daily,
As we sing while marching to eternity.

Along the way, everyone can shout:
Glory to God, He redeemed me!
Glory to God, He set me free!
Glory to God, He died for humanity!
Glory to God, He sealed my destiny!

PATIENCE

Patience, 'tis long suffering,
And pain that's so enduring,
But victory will soon be here,
For God truly answers prayer.

Patience 'tis long suffering,
I must be steadfast and keep praying;
Even when my hopes are low
I'll trust God and wait for tomorrow.

Patience, 'tis bitter, not sweet,
'Cause sometimes I can't even sleep,
In the dawn of morn I lie awake,
And pray about what's at stake.

Patience, 'tis tolerance and endurance,
But God gives words of assurance –
"Have patience, no matter what the circumstance,
For the end result is not by chance."

Patience, 'tis a "marvelous virtue",
It requires much fortitude and
Builds character and a good attitude,
Till God's timing sees me through.

Patience, 'tis long suffering,
But victory, it will always bring
In God's own time, not thine;
Patience will always be mine.

Have patience! My friend,
It will sustain you to the end.

TIME, OH TIME!

Oh! Did you hear the clock chime?
It tells me that I still have time
To prepare for a long journey
To a garden-state of beautiful memory.

Oh! I look at the huge clock,
As the pendulum swings —
Tick-tock, tick-tock,
It moves to and fro with no haste,
Yet time, man seems to hastily chase.

Oh! The clock continues to chime,
And time refuses to wait on no man,
Time, Oh time! When did it all begin?
It's by the "King of Ancient Time!"

Oh! Since time refuses to wait,
I must get ready now before it's too late,
If I'm to reach that beautiful garden-state,
That has flowers and fruits of every taste.

UNITED IN CHRIST

United in Christ we set our hearts,
Each day as we do our tasks.
Others must see God's love in us,
For it's the only thing that will last.

United in Christ we cannot fail,
For God leads us through this life,
And no matter what's at stake,
He sees the journey we undertake.

United in Christ we're on solid ground,
Even though life's tempests round us mount,
God is the Master with a mighty hand,
And storms obey at His command.

United in Christ we are not alone,
As we try to reach our heavenly home,
God will be our Guide and Friend
Who'll see us through to the very end.

Triumphantly in Christ we forward go,
Putting our faith and hope on things above,
As we unite in love and harmony,
That will take us to eternity.

WALKING THE STREETS

While walking the street of Abandonment,
I saw the Avenue of Discouragement,
But afar off was the Road of Discernment,
Lined with trees so magnificent.

I looked up in amazement and saw the Omnipotent,
He whispered, "My child, I'm Omnipresent;
Come, let me hold your hand,
I'll walk you through this land."

I said, "Oh Master! Please don't let me go,
I need your guiding hand for sure,
As I walk these streets here below,
Lord, save me when life's billows roar."

This journey will soon be o'er,
Over yonder, I'll walk streets paved with gold,
And sing, "Glory, glory, Hallelujah,
To the Lamb, my Shepherd, my Savior."

WINGS TO FLY

If only I had wings to fly
Beyond the mysteries of the sky,
I'd see angels in action,
Carrying out God's Master Plan.

Instead, I must walk earth's journey,
With King Jesus by my side,
Knowing He directs each mile,
And waits for me beyond the sky.

Each day I'm getting closer,
And each burden gets lighter,
When I pour my heart out in prayer,
Jesus assures me that He is near.

My life is in God's hand,
As I labor in this strange land;
God has already designed a plan,
That will get me to "Heavenly Canaan."

(1986: My first written poem)

CPSIA information can be obtained at www.ICGtesting.com
Printed in the USA
BVOW020715041012

302098BV00001B/12/P